VA LOAN
MASTERY

THE HIDDEN POWER
OF OWNERSHIP AND
ASSUMPTIONS

DEEP-DIVE INTO THE MOST
MISUNDERSTOOD WEALTH-BUILDING
TOOL FOR MILITARY BUYERS

ASK ANTWAUN

VA Loan Mastery

The Hidden Power Of Ownership
And Assumptions

ISBN: 979-8-9936505-2-4

Published by AskAntwaun Media

All inquiries: AskAntwaun@gmail.com
Printed in the United States of America

Book Design by Williams DocuPrep
www.williamsdocuprep.com

Table of Contents

Acknowledgements

To every service member, veteran, and family who's ever wondered if financial freedom was really possible, this is for you. You've sacrificed, served, and endured. You deserve more than stability; you deserve prosperity.

To the agents, lenders, and mentors who continue to serve our military community through education and integrity, thank you. You make the difference between a buyer and a believer.

And to my family, for your patience, support, and faith during every late night, long call, and new project, you're the "why" behind every word.

Introduction

The Most Misunderstood Military Benefit

When I bought my first home using my VA loan, I wasn't in uniform anymore. I had already transitioned out of the Army and was working as a Department of Defense contractor. For more than a decade in service, I rented everywhere I went: Georgia, Korea, Virginia, New York, and Hawaii. Every PCS felt temporary, so I treated it that way. Owning a home? That was something I would do later.

Like a lot of service members, I didn't think of real estate as a strategy. I saw it as stability, something to chase once the moving stopped. What I didn't realize was that I'd spent 13 years funding someone else's stability while holding one of the most powerful financial benefits in America in my back pocket: the VA loan.

When I finally bought, I thought I understood it. Zero down. No PMI. Decent rate. Cool. I figured that was the benefit. I used it, checked the box, and moved on.

It took years in real estate to realize that the VA loan isn't just a way to buy a home, it's a wealth tool. The truth is, nobody ever explained that part. Not during briefings, not from the lenders, not even from other agents. Nobody said, "Hey, this is how you can use your VA loan to own multiple properties, let someone else assume your rate, and grow your portfolio while still serving."

Instead, we got the usual myths:
- "You can only use it once."
- "You can't rent out a VA home."
- "You can't hold more than one at a time."

Every one of those statements is wrong. For years, I didn't know that entitlement could be restored and re-used. I didn't know you could carry multiple VA loans at once if you structured them properly. And I definitely didn't know you could sell your home with your rate attached and turn that into a marketing advantage worth thousands of dollars.

I learned those lessons the long way, through experience, through clients, and through trial and error. But when it clicked, it changed everything.

That's what this book is about.

It's not about rules; it's about strategy. It's about understanding how to make your VA loan work for you long after your DD-214 is signed. You've already earned the benefit. Now it's time to master it.

Because the VA loan isn't just a military perk; it's a blueprint for ownership. Used right, it can fund your first home, your first rental, your first assumption sale, and even your first step into financial freedom.

You don't need to earn more. You just need to use it better. Because the VA loan isn't a one-time opportunity; it's a lifetime advantage.

And once you understand that you'll stop seeing it as paperwork...and start seeing it as power.

Chapter 1

The Myth and the Mastery

When it comes to the VA loan, the biggest challenge isn't qualification; it's education. The truth is, most of us never really learned what we were holding. I used to believe all the same things everyone else did:

- "You can only use it once."

- "You can't rent out a VA-financed home."

- "You can't use your VA loan if you already own another property."

And when I say I believed those things, I mean I built my financial decisions around them.

I rented for years because I thought buying during active duty wasn't worth it. I figured, "Why buy if I'll have to move again in a few years?" I told myself that was the smart play: flexible, simple, and no strings attached. But looking back now, that mindset cost me more than I realized.

See, the VA loan isn't restrictive; it's leverageable. It's not a single-use coupon. It's a lifelong key to ownership. I just didn't know how to use it.

The Myth Cycle

The military is great at repetition. We drill it, brief it, and repeat it until it sticks. But when it comes to financial literacy, that repetition often spreads misinformation.

Someone hears a rumor in the barracks about the VA loan. They repeat it at the motor pool. Then someone else tells it at the next duty station. Over time, that rumor becomes fact, and that fact becomes F.E.A.R.: **False Evidence Appearing Real.**

I've met soldiers, sailors, airmen, and Marines who were terrified to even use their VA loan because of something a buddy told them five years earlier. And who can blame them? No one wants to make a financial mistake they don't understand.

- So they rent.

- Year after year.

- Base after base.

- Paycheck after paycheck.

And that's how hundreds of thousands of service members miss out on one of the greatest wealth-building opportunities of their lives.

My Wake-Up Call

For me, the wake-up call didn't come in uniform; it came after separation. When I finally started working in real estate, I realized how many people around me were using their VA benefits like chess pieces, not checkboxes.

They weren't just buying homes; they were buying positions. They understood that the VA loan wasn't just about affordability. It was about control.

- Control of your rate.

- Control of your terms.

- Control of your path to financial independence.

They knew what I didn't: that this wasn't a one-and-done loan. It was a lifetime of opportunity hidden in plain sight.

From Myth to Mastery

Mastery doesn't come from doing something once. It comes from understanding how it works. That's where the shift happens from thinking like a borrower to thinking like an investor.

When you start looking at your VA loan not as a benefit but as a strategy, your decisions change. You stop asking, *"Can I use it?"* and start asking, *"How can I use it better?"*

That's the mastery. Because once you understand what this loan really allows—entitlement reuse, partial restorations, multi-property leverage, and assumable rates—you stop playing defense and start playing offense.

The VA loan isn't a handout. It's a financial weapon. The question is, are you trained to use it?

Golden Nugget Tips

- **Myth #1:** "You can only use it once."

  Truth: You can restore and reuse your entitlement as many times as you want, even while holding multiple properties under certain conditions.

- **Myth #2:** "You can't rent out your VA home."

  Truth: You must occupy it initially, but after that, you can rent it out and build passive income as long as you meet the occupancy requirement upfront.

- **Myth #3:** "You can't have two VA loans."

  Truth: You can if your remaining entitlement and county loan limits support it.

The difference between myth and mastery isn't access; it's *understanding*.

Chapter 2

Understanding Entitlement

If the VA loan were a car, *entitlement* would be the engine. You can't move without it, and you can't go far if you don't understand how it runs.

Here's the truth: most service members who say, "I've already used my VA loan," don't actually understand what that means. They think entitlement is a one-time ticket: use it or lose it. But that's not how it works at all.

Entitlement isn't something you use up. It's something you *leverage*. And like any form of leverage, if you know how to manage it, you can reuse it, restore it, and even stack it.

What Is VA Entitlement?

In simple terms, *entitlement* is the amount of money the Department of Veterans Affairs guarantees to your lender on your behalf.

When you buy a home with a VA loan, the VA promises the lender that if you default, the VA will repay a portion of the loan, usually up to 25%. That promise gives the lender confidence to offer you incredible terms: no down payment, competitive interest rates, and no private mortgage insurance (PMI).

So, entitlement is not your money. It's your *backing power*. And that backing power can be used over and over again as long as you manage it wisely.

Full Entitlement vs. Partial Entitlement

There are two main types of entitlement:

1. **Full Entitlement** – You've either never used your VA loan, or you've sold the home and paid off your previous VA loan completely. You're eligible for the full VA guarantee amount (currently 25% of your county loan limit).

2. **Partial Entitlement** – You still have a portion of your entitlement tied up in another property with an active VA loan. You can still buy another home, but how much you can borrow with no down payment depends on how much entitlement you have left.

How Entitlement Really Works — Plain Talk Example

Let's make this real.

Meet Staff Sergeant Miller. He bought his first home in Georgia for $250,000 using his VA loan. The VA guaranteed 25% of that loan, or $62,500. That's the portion of his entitlement that's now being used.

Here's what most people don't realize: every qualified veteran has a total entitlement that allows the VA to guarantee up to 25% of the conforming loan limit in their county.

In 2024, most counties have a limit of $766,550, meaning the VA will back up to $191,637.50 (25% of that limit). That's your *total entitlement power*.

So in Miller's case:

- His Georgia home used $62,500 of that.
- He still has $129,137.50 of entitlement left.

Now Miller gets orders to Hawaii, where the county loan limit is much higher — $1,149,825. That means the VA will back up to $287,456.25 in that area (25% of the limit).

When Miller applies for a new VA loan in Hawaii, the lender checks how much entitlement he still has left—$129,137.50. Since the VA guarantees 25% of every VA loan, the lender multiplies that number by four.

That means Miller can buy a home for up to roughly

$516,550 with *zero down*, even while still owning his Georgia home. If he wants to buy a home priced higher than that, he just needs a small down payment to make up the difference. Not a dealbreaker, just math.

In Plain English

- You don't lose your VA loan benefit when you buy a home.

- You can own multiple VA-financed homes at once.

- Your remaining buying power depends on how much entitlement is still tied up in your other property.

- Selling or paying off a VA-backed loan restores your full entitlement automatically.

This is why understanding entitlement is so powerful. It's not about limits; it's about *leverage*.

Restoring Your Entitlement

You can restore your entitlement in three ways:

1. **Sell your home and pay off the VA loan in full.**
   Once that loan is cleared, your entitlement resets automatically.

2. **Allow another eligible veteran to assume your VA loan.**

If they substitute their entitlement for yours, your eligibility is restored the moment the assumption is complete.

3. **Request a one-time restoration without selling.**

    The VA allows this once if you've paid off the loan in full but still own the home as long as it's no longer financed with a VA loan.

Golden Nugget Tips

- **You never lose entitlement**; you just need to restore it.

- **You can have multiple VA loans at once**, as long as your remaining entitlement and county loan limits support it.

- **Bonus entitlement** = more buying power in high-cost markets like Hawaii, California, and D.C.

Entitlement is the engine behind every VA loan, but it's the *zero-down power* that really makes it move.

Chapter 3

The Zero Down Advantage

When most people hear "zero down," they think it sounds too good to be true. Free money? No way. But here's the real story: *it's not free; it's leverage.*

The VA loan's zero-down feature isn't charity; it's *strategy.* It rewards your service by removing the biggest barrier to homeownership, the down payment, while giving you a financial weapon that most civilians don't have access to. Used wisely, it's a wealth accelerator. Used recklessly, it's a trap.

Why Zero Down Matters

For most Americans, the biggest obstacle to buying a home isn't credit; it's cash. Saving up tens of thousands of dollars for a down payment can take years. But the VA loan eliminates that wall entirely. And it's not just about *getting in the door.* Zero down means your cash stays **liquid,** ready for the next move, the next PCS, or the next opportunity.

Liquidity is power. Because cash in your pocket gives you flexibility, and flexibility is what separates the struggling from the strategic.

How It Works: VA vs. FHA vs. Conventional

Let's put some real numbers behind this. Imagine you're buying a **$500,000** home.

Loan Type	Down Payment	Interest Rate	PMI / MIP	Monthly Payment (Principal + Interest + Insurance)	Notes
VA Loan	$0	6.25%	$0	~$3,080	No PMI, full financing, lowest overall cost
FHA Loan	$17,500 (3.5%)	6.75%	~$350	~$3,420	MIP required for life of loan (unless 10%+ down)
Conventional Loan	$25,000 (5%)	7.00%	~$275	~$3,480	PMI until 20% equity reached

Right away, you can see the VA advantage lower monthly cost, no PMI, and you keep your savings intact. But the real difference shows up over time.

Five-Year Cost & Equity Comparison

Here's what happens after **5 years** in that same $500,000 home. We'll assume 3% annual home appreciation (modest) and include monthly savings over 60 months.

Loan Type	Total Cash Invested Up-front	Approx. Total Paid (5 Years)	Est. Home Value After 5 Years	Approx. Loan Balance After 5 Years	Home Equity	Net Wealth Position
VA Loan	$0	$184,800	$579,637	$456,000	$123,637	$123,637 gain, $0 upfront
FHA Loan	$17,500	$205,200	$579,637	$458,000	$121,637	$104,137 (after subtracting down payment)
Conv Loan	$25,000	$208,800	$579,637	$457,000	$122,637	$97,637 (after subtracting down payment)

Right away, you can see the VA advantage: lower monthly cost, no PMI, and you keep your savings intact. But the real difference shows up over time.

Five-Year Cost & Equity Comparison

Here's what happens after 5 years in that same

$500,000 home. We'll assume 3% annual home appreciation (modest) and include monthly savings over 60 months.

Result:

Even with *zero down*, the VA buyer ends up with the highest net position after 5 years, thanks to lower payments and no PMI dragging on growth. And that's before factoring in what they did with the cash they kept, like upgrades, a reserve fund, or seed money for another property.

The Real Power of Leverage

When people hear "zero down," they think it means "no ownership." But the truth is, it means faster ownership. Because while others are saving for a down payment, you're already building equity, appreciation, and experience.

If you saved $25,000 for a conventional down payment and spent 3 years trying to stack it up, your money wouldn't just be sitting. It would be *missing* all the appreciation you could've earned by owning sooner.

That's what I call "lost equity," and it's one of the most expensive financial mistakes service members make.

Zero Down ≠ No Risk

Here's the other side of the coin: Leverage only works when used responsibly. If you buy too much house or move too often without a plan, zero down can become zero equity fast. That's why discipline matters. Use the zero-down advantage *strategically*, not emotionally.

Ask yourself:

- Can I hold this property long enough to gain equity?
- Could I rent it out if I got orders next year?
- Is this purchase setting me up for my next one?

That's how you turn "zero down" from an opportunity into a system.

Zero Down and the PCS Game

Here's where it gets powerful: your PCS orders are *built-in opportunities* to use zero down over and over again. Each move gives you a new market, a new BAH rate, and a new shot at equity.

You can buy, live, rent, and repeat stacking ownership like dominoes across duty stations. Every civilian has to grind for years to buy a second home. You get handed the opportunity every few years. Zero down doesn't just help you buy your first house; it helps you buy your *next one*.

- **Zero down doesn't mean no cost.** You'll still pay closing costs, but you can negotiate seller credits or use lender incentives to cover them.

- **Keep your cash working.** Don't spend what you saved on the deal; use it as emergency or investment capital.

- **Equity compounds.** The earlier you start owning, the longer appreciation has to work for you.

The VA loan's zero-down power isn't about skipping the line; it's about changing your lane. Because while everyone else is saving to buy, you're already owning, building, and setting up your next move.

And one of the most strategic ways to maximize that power isn't just through buying; it's through letting *someone else* take it over. That's right. Someone can step into your VA loan, keep your low rate, and even put cash in your pocket in the process. Welcome to the Assumption Advantage, the heart of the VA loan strategy most people still don't understand.

Chapter 4

The Assumption Advantage

If the zero-down benefit is the spark of the VA loan, assumptions are the flame nobody sees coming. The VA loan assumption might be the most powerful and misunderstood feature in real estate today. It's the tool that can literally save or make someone six figures over time, yet 9 out of 10 buyers (and agents) don't even know it exists. So, let's fix that.

What Is a VA Loan Assumption?

A VA loan assumption means a new buyer takes over the *existing loan* on a property—the balance, the rate, the terms, everything. That means if a seller has a loan at 2.75%, and today's rates are 6.75%, a buyer can assume that same loan and keep that rate.

Think about that for a second. That's not just a savings; that's leverage built into the loan itself. The buyer doesn't have to refinance or requalify for a new mortgage. They simply *step into* the seller's existing financing.

Who Can Assume a VA Loan?

Here's the part that most people get wrong: you don't have to be a veteran to assume a VA loan.

There are two main types of assumptions:

1. **VA-to-VA Assumption:**

   The buyer is a qualified veteran using their VA eligibility.

   - Entitlement from the buyer *replaces* the seller's entitlement.

   - The seller's entitlement is **restored in full** once the assumption closes.

2. **Non-VA Assumption:**

   The buyer is *not* a veteran.

   - The VA allows this as long as the buyer qualifies financially and the loan servicer approves.

   - The seller's entitlement remains **tied up** until the buyer pays off the loan or refinances it.

In either case, the buyer must meet the same credit, income, and debt-to-income (DTI) standards that a new borrower would. But if approved, they inherit a loan that's already at a below-market rate, and that's where the magic happens.

The Math Behind the Savings

- Let's say a home has a $600,000 assumable loan at 2.75% with 25 years remaining.

- A new $600,000 loan today at 6.75% would have a principal and interest payment around $3,890/month.

- The assumed loan, at 2.75%, would be $2,450/month.

- That's a monthly savings of $1,440, or over $17,000 a year.

Over just five years, the buyer saves $85,000+, and over the life of the loan, the difference can exceed $250,000. And that's before factoring in appreciation or equity growth.

Now imagine being the seller. If your home has a 2.75% rate in a 7% market, that loan is an asset. You're not just selling a home; you're selling a *payment*.

Why Sellers Should Care

In a high-rate environment, homes with assumable loans become premium listings. They attract more buyers and can often command stronger prices or fewer days on the market. That's why understanding how to market an assumable loan is just as important as having one.

When I market an assumable listing, I'm not selling square footage; I'm selling *affordability*. That means I highlight the rate, the payment, and the potential savings upfront.

For example:

> *"Assumable VA Loan at 2.75%! Save over $1,400/month compared to current rates."*

That one line can turn a curious buyer into a serious one.

Real-World Example: How One Buyer Saved Six Figures

I had a couple who assumed a VA loan on a property listed at $915,000. The seller's remaining loan balance was $685,000 at a 2.375% rate. Rather than taking out a new mortgage, my buyers paid the difference of about $230,000 as their "assumption gap."

Their new monthly payment came out to around $3,200, while similar homes at market rates were over $5,100/month. That's $1,900 monthly, $22,800 a year in savings. Over just five years, they'll save more than $110,000 in payments alone.

And when rates drop and other buyers refinance, their home becomes even more valuable because they're already sitting on a rate that others can only dream of.

Key Terms to Know

Term	Definition
Assumption Gap	The difference between the home's price and the remaining loan balance. Buyer must pay this in cash or financing.
Entitlement Substitution	When a VA buyer replaces the seller's entitlement, freeing the seller's benefit.
Release of Liability	The official document from the lender that removes the seller from responsibility after the assumption.
Servicer Approval	Every assumption must be approved by the loan's servicer (Freedom, PennyMac, etc.). This can take weeks to months.

What to Watch Out For

- **Timeline:** Assumptions take longer than standard sales, often 60–90 days.

- **Seller Risk:** If the buyer is *not* a veteran, your entitlement stays tied up until they refinance or pay off the loan.

- **Servicer Bottlenecks:** Many servicers are still

catching up on backlog, which can delay approval.

- **Buyer Qualification:** The buyer must still meet income and credit standards; assumptions aren't automatic.

But for both sides, when done right, they're worth every minute.

Why This Strategy Matters

When rates rise, assumptions shine. When rates fall, they become the ultimate selling tool. Either way, understanding how to spot, market, and negotiate assumable loans gives you an edge 90% of agents don't have. It's not theory; it's strategy.

The Assumption Advantage turns your VA loan into a *transferable asset*, not just a mortgage. And that's how military homeowners can win, no matter the market.

Golden Nugget Tips

- **Your loan is an asset.** Keep documentation and servicing info; you never know when your low rate will become valuable.

- **Always verify assumption eligibility early.** Contact your servicer before listing or offering.

- **For buyers:** Don't overlook assumption listings; they can save you six figures and years of interest.

- **For sellers:** Even non-veterans can assume your VA loan; you just need approval and a release of liability if possible.

Your first VA loan got you into the game. Your assumption strategy helps you play it smarter. But what if you could play multiple boards at once using your entitlement to own *more than one property* at the same time? That's where most people get it wrong... and where your next advantage begins.

Chapter 5

Stacking VA Loans (Yes, You Can)

If there's one line I've heard more than any other when it comes to the VA loan, it's *"You can only have one VA loan at a time."* Wrong. That single sentence has probably stopped more military families from building wealth than any other myth out there. Because the truth is you can absolutely have more than one VA loan at the same time. You just need to understand *how*.

The Myth vs. The Math

The VA loan doesn't limit you to one property. It limits you by something called entitlement, your piece of the VA's guarantee pie. The VA guarantees 25% of your loan amount. That guarantee is what lets lenders offer 100% financing with no PMI. You're allocated a certain amount of entitlement based on county loan limits. So, when people say, "You can't have two VA loans," what they really mean is, "You don't have enough remaining entitlement for a second full loan." But that's where smart structuring comes in.

Breaking Down Entitlement

Let's make this simple with numbers. The VA's *basic entitlement* is $36,000. That number sounds small, but it's just the foundation. The real cap is based on your county's conforming loan limit.

Here's how it works:

The VA guarantees up to 25% of your county's loan limit. So if your county limit is $977,500 (like in Honolulu County), that means the VA can back up to $244,375 of entitlement on your behalf. That's enough to cover 100% financing on a $977,500 home. If your first VA loan only used part of that, you can still use the rest.

Example: Two VA Loans at Once

Let's say you bought your first home in Texas for $400,000 using your VA loan. The VA guaranteed 25% of that, or $100,000 of entitlement. Then you get PCS orders to Hawaii, where the loan limit is $977,500.

That means you still have $144,375 of entitlement left ($244,375 total minus the $100,000 used). To find your new maximum VA loan without a down payment, multiply the remaining entitlement by 4: $144,375 × 4 = $577,500. So, you can purchase a new home up to $577,500 with no down payment, *even while keeping the first VA loan.*

If you want to buy above that, you just make up the difference with a small down payment, not 20%, just enough to bridge the gap.

How the VA Sees It

The VA doesn't mind you owning two properties; they just care that the new one is your primary residence. That means you must intend to live there full-time when you close.

What happens later? Renting out your previous home, converting it to an investment, or holding both is allowed, as long as you originally occupied each property as your main home when purchased.

That's the PCS advantage. Every move can become another property if you plan it right.

The PCS Stacking Strategy

Here's what this looks like in real life:

1. **PCS #1:** Buy a home at your duty station using your VA loan — $400,000 at 3.25%.

2. **PCS #2:** Get orders to a new location. Keep your old home and rent it out for $2,500/month.

   Use remaining entitlement to buy again at $575,000 this time at 4.5%.

   Result: You now own two homes, both appreciating, both paid down by tenants and BAH.

Over time, appreciation, equity paydown, and rent increases compound. This is how everyday service members quietly build 7-figure portfolios while still serving.

Stacking in High-Cost Areas

In places like Hawaii, San Diego, or D.C., you may hit entitlement limits faster. That's where strategic combinations come into play:

- **Partial entitlement** + small down payment—bridge the gap.

- **VA + Conventional combo loan**—split financing to keep VA usage clean.

- **Sell or refinance the old home**—restore entitlement completely and start fresh.

Each of these can be customized based on your PCS timeline, cash position, and market.

Entitlement Restoration vs. Reuse

When you sell a home and the VA loan is paid in full, your entitlement resets. That's called restoration. When you keep the home and buy another, you're reusing your remaining entitlement. Both are powerful tools, and knowing which to use when determines how fast you can scale.

Real Talk: Why This Matters

Here's the key:

The VA loan isn't a one-time benefit; it's a revolving door of opportunity. Every PCS can be a stepping stone. Every entitlement reset can be a relaunch.

You just have to stop thinking of your VA loan as a "use it and lose it" benefit and start treating it like what it really is: a lifelong investment weapon.

Golden Nugget Tips

- **Check your COE (Certificate of Eligibility)** early. It shows how much entitlement is currently used and what's left.

- **Remember your county limits.** They change every year, and they can expand your buying power significantly.

- **Stack strategically.** Think "PCS-to-PCS," not

"house-to-house."

- **Sell when it makes sense.** Sometimes restoring full entitlement is the best move for your next deal.

Stacking VA loans turns your military journey into a map of wealth creation. Every move, another brick in the wall. But once you've built that wall, the next step is protecting and optimizing it. That means learning to use your loan not just to buy, but to *refine* your position, whether that's lowering your rate, freeing equity, or improving your cash flow.

Chapter 6

Refinancing the Smart Way

The word "refinance" usually makes people think of starting over with a new loan, new fees, and a new term. But when used strategically, refinancing isn't a restart. It's a *refinement.*

It's how you take the home you already own and make it work *harder* for you, whether that means lowering your payment, pulling out cash for the next opportunity, or positioning yourself for your next PCS.

The key is knowing why you're refinancing, not just that you can.

The Three Refinance Paths

There are three main ways to refinance your VA loan, and each serves a very different purpose.

1. **IRRRL (Interest Rate Reduction Refinance Loan)**

The most common and the most misunderstood. The IRRRL, pronounced "Earl," is a streamline refinance designed to lower your interest rate or move from an adjustable-rate mortgage (ARM) to a fixed one.

- No appraisal (in most cases)
- No income verification
- No occupancy requirement. Perfect if you've already PCS'd
- Minimal closing costs (and often rolled into the loan)

  The catch? You must already have a VA loan. You can't pull cash out with an IRRRL, but you can lower your payment, free up monthly cash flow, and stabilize your budget.

  Example:

  If you bought a $500,000 home at 6.25% and rates drop to 4.75%, refinancing could reduce your payment by nearly **$450/month;** that's over **$5,000 a year** in freed-up capital.

2. **VA Cash-Out Refinance**

This is the power move. It lets you tap into your home's equity, the difference between what your home is worth and what you owe, to pull out cash for other uses.

You can use that equity to:

- Pay off high-interest debt.
- Fund another down payment (for stacking or an investment property).
- Renovate your current home.
- Build reserves or an emergency fund.
- But there's a difference between using equity to grow and using it to consume.

Using it to grow means reinvesting it into assets, another property, education, or income-producing improvements.

Using it to consume means funding vacations, cars, or short-term luxuries that leave you with a higher loan balance and no return.

If it doesn't multiply your money, it's not an investment; it's a withdrawal from your future.

3. **HELOC (Home Equity Line of Credit)**

The hybrid tool. A HELOC is a revolving line of credit secured by your home's equity. Think of it like a credit card with a much lower interest rate. It gives you the flexibility to draw when needed, repay, and reuse.

Great for:

- Renovations or repairs.
- Temporary bridge funding between PCS moves.
- Quick liquidity without full refinancing.

Just remember: HELOCs often carry variable rates, which means your payment can change over time. They're best for short-term or strategic use, not long-term reliance.

Equity: The Hidden Engine

Every mortgage payment you make is quietly building equity wealth that belongs to you. Refinancing is how you decide *when* and *how* to deploy it. The key question isn't, "Can I pull it out?" It's "Should I?"

Because equity is like stored energy. Once you use it, you have to rebuild it, and that takes time.

Example:

If your home is worth $700,000 and you owe $500,000, you have $200,000 in equity. Pulling out $100,000 might sound great, but that's half your stored wealth gone overnight. Ask yourself: will this move help me grow another $200,000 or just make today easier?

Refinancing and the PCS Cycle

PCS moves make refinancing opportunities appear naturally. Why? Because each new market has new rates, new values, and new timing.

Here's the PCS refinance rhythm used by savvy military investors:

1. **Buy at the start of a tour.**

2. **Refi mid-tour** if rates drop, stabilize the property, or access cash.

3. **PCS out and rent.** The refi lowers the payment, increasing your rental cash flow.

4. **Buy again at your new duty station.**

It's not luck; it's a system. Refinancing isn't random; it's a timing move in the broader wealth playbook.

The Discipline Factor

Refinancing is one of those things that can make you rich or bury you in debt, depending on how you play it. The difference comes down to discipline.

- Refinancing to lower your rate or free up capital for another property? Smart.

- Refinancing to buy a truck, take a trip, or "get ahead on bills"? Costly.

A refinance should strengthen your financial position, not just change your monthly payment.

Golden Nugget Tips

- **Refinance when it makes math sense.** A rule of thumb: drop your rate by 0.75% or more to justify the costs.

- **Know your break-even point.** Divide closing costs by monthly savings to see when you'll recoup the expense.

- **Equity is leverage, not income.** Use it to multiply assets, not cover lifestyle.

- **Check eligibility.** IRRRLs require an existing VA loan; cash-out refis can apply to any existing mortgage type.

Refinancing is the quiet art of repositioning, not resetting. It's how you make sure every dollar in your mortgage continues to serve your goals. And when it's time to sell, there's one final play most people never consider: you can actually use your VA loan to attract buyers and often sell faster for more.

Chapter 7

Using Your VA Loan to Attract Buyers

When rates go up, sellers start worrying, "Will my home still sell fast?" "Will buyers even qualify now that payments are higher?" But VA homeowners who understand their advantage don't worry; they market differently. Because what they have isn't just a home. It's a *payment plan worth keeping*.

When you have a VA loan with a low interest rate, your mortgage isn't just financing; it's a financial asset. And that asset can make your property sell faster, attract more buyers, and even sell *above market value*.

Why Your Loan Is Part of the Sale

In a normal sale, buyers shop based on price. But when interest rates rise, price becomes less important than monthly payment. Buyers don't ask, "How much is the house?" They ask, "How much is the payment?"

That's where your VA loan can change the game.

If you have an assumable VA loan at 2.5%, and new loans are at 6.5%, a buyer can take over your rate, saving hundreds or even thousands per month. That difference in monthly affordability can make your property the most desirable on the block.

Real Example: The 2.75% Power Play

A seller in Ewa Beach had a VA loan at **2.75%** with a remaining balance of $620,000. At current market rates, that same balance would cost a new buyer about $4,100/month in principal and interest.

By assuming the seller's loan, the buyer's payment dropped to $2,530/month. That's a monthly savings of $1,570, or almost $19,000 per year.

Even though the buyer had to bring $200,000 cash to cover the difference between the sale price and loan balance (the "assumption gap"), the math still worked out beautifully.

Why? Because they bought *affordability*. That cash didn't vanish, it became instant equity. And for the seller? They sold faster and above list price.

Marketing the Assumption

Here's the truth: Most buyers and agents don't fully understand assumptions, and that's your edge.

When marketing your home:

- **Lead with the rate, not the price.**

  Example: "Assumable VA Loan at 2.75%! Save over $1,500/month vs. today's market rate."

- **Explain the opportunity clearly.**

  Highlight how assumption eligibility works for *both* veterans and non-veterans.

- **Show the math.**

  Include an estimated payment comparison in your listing remarks. When done right, your home attracts not just more attention but *the right kind* of attention. Buyers who understand financing see value where others see price.

How to Make Your Loan Assumable

If you're a VA homeowner planning to sell, here's how to prepare:

1. Contact your servicer early.

Ask if your loan is assumable (most VA loans are) and what documents they require for approval.

2. Confirm your release of liability.

Once the buyer assumes your loan, you'll want official confirmation that you're no longer financially responsible.

3. Keep your documentation handy.

Loan statements, payment history, and any correspondence make the process smoother.

4. Work with an agent who understands VA assumptions.

The assumption process isn't difficult; it's just specific. Experience matters.

VA Assumptions for Non-VA Buyers

Here's the best-kept secret: Non-veterans can also assume VA loans. That's right; you don't need to have served to take over a VA loan. The difference is that the seller's entitlement remains tied to the property until the loan is paid off or refinanced.

But for sellers who have equity or plan to buy their next home using a different loan type, that's not a dealbreaker. It's often worth it to unlock a higher sale price or faster closing.

The Psychology of the Payment

When rates rise, buyers feel priced out. An assumable loan gives them *permission* to dream again because the payment feels possible. That emotional trigger is powerful. You're not just offering a house; you're offering hope that homeownership is still within reach. And that's what sells homes, especially in shifting markets.

The Strategic Seller Mindset

The goal isn't just to sell; it's to *leverage the sale*. If your home has a low-rate VA loan:

- You can market the rate as part of your home's value.

- You can create urgency with buyers who understand long-term savings.

- You can command stronger offers because affordability has tangible value.

Once you sell, you can restore your VA entitlement and reuse it at your next duty station, starting the cycle all over again. That's what makes the VA loan not just a benefit but a *business tool*.

Golden Nugget Tips

- **Always advertise the rate.** It's your biggest

marketing asset.

- **Request a release of liability.** Protect your entitlement and your credit.

- **Educate your agent.** Make sure they understand the assumption process and how to position it.

- **Think beyond this sale.** Restoring your entitlement is step one for your next move.

A low-rate VA loan isn't just something you keep; it's something you can *sell.* It's your silent advantage in a noisy market and the difference between *listing a home* and *leveraging an asset.*

But selling isn't the end of the journey. For those who stay in the game, it's the bridge to the next level, owning not just a home, but a portfolio.

Chapter 8

The Investor's Playbook

There's a moment when every military homeowner realizes something powerful: *"Wait... I could keep this place and buy another."* That's the spark, the shift from *homeowner* to *investor*.

It's the moment you stop seeing your PCS as a disruption and start seeing it as a wealth strategy. The VA loan makes that possible. not just once, but again and again. Every move, every tour, and every set of orders can become part of your portfolio story.

The PCS-to-Profit Strategy

Every PCS comes with three automatic advantages:

1. Guaranteed housing income (your BAH).

2. Frequent relocation opportunities.

3. Tax-advantaged financing benefits.

Those three things, when combined intentionally,

are the building blocks of a rental portfolio.

Let's walk through how it works.

Step 1: Buy Smart, Not Sentimental

When you buy your first home, don't just think about living in it; think about *leaving* it.

Ask yourself:

- Will this rent easily when I PCS?

- Is it close to base, schools, and main routes?

- Does the payment make sense for the local rental market?

If the answer is yes, you've bought what I call a PCS-proof property: a home that's both livable and rentable. When you move, you don't need to sell it. You just hand the keys to your first tenant instead of a buyer.

Step 2: Convert BAH into a Business Model

BAH is more than a housing allowance; it's your built-in cash-flow source. When you buy a home using your VA loan, your BAH covers the mortgage, often with room to spare if you buy strategically. After you PCS, that same property can generate rent that exceeds your mortgage payment. That's the PCS flip: you move out, but the income stays behind.

Example:

You purchase a home for $450,000 with a $2,800/month payment. Three years later, your new BAH covers the next home, and the old one rents for $3,300/month.

That's $500/month in cash flow, or $6,000 a year, while tenants pay down your principal and the home continues to appreciate. Do this every PCS, and you'll have a growing, diversified portfolio before you retire from service.

Step 3: Protect Your Entitlement (and Use It Wisely)

You don't need to sell your first VA-financed home to buy another. You can use the remaining entitlement to purchase your next property. When you eventually sell, that portion of entitlement is restored, giving you a clean slate to repeat the process.

This cycle of *buy, PCS, rent, and buy again* is how service members quietly build portfolios across multiple states without ever using traditional investor financing.

Step 4: Manage from Anywhere

The biggest hesitation most service members have is, "What if I can't manage a rental from across the country?" You don't have to.

There are systems for that:

- **Property managers** handle tenants, repairs, and rent collection.

- **Online tools** like Buildium, AppFolio, or Ren-tRedi let you track payments and maintenance.

- **Military networks** at each base can help you find trusted local vendors.

The goal isn't to manage properties; it's to own systems that manage properties for you. Once that's in place, every PCS becomes another business expansion, not another goodbye.

Step 5: Use Equity, Don't Drain It

When you own multiple VA-financed homes, equity becomes your biggest asset. But it's also the easiest to misuse. Instead of cashing out for lifestyle purchases, use your equity as leverage:

- Fund down payments for the next home.

- Pay off high-interest debt.

- Add value to current properties (like renovations or ADUs).

Each move should position you stronger, not just

wealthier on paper, but freer in reality.

The Math of Momentum

Here's what this looks like over time for a career service member:

PCS Move	Home Price	Pay-ment	Rent After PCS	Monthly Cash Flow	Portfolio Value
1	$400,000	$2,600	$3,000	$400	$400,000
2	$475,000	$3,100	$3,400	$300	$875,000
3	$550,000	$3,600	$4,000	$400	$1.4M

By year 12, your tenants have paid down tens of thousands in principal, and appreciation could easily add another $300,000–$500,000 in equity. All from simply buying smart every time you moved.

Building a Military-Grade Portfolio

The best part of this strategy? It doesn't require becoming a full-time investor. You don't need to flip homes or chase Airbnb trends. You just need to make *every PCS count.*

Over time, your "orders" become your roadmap:

- Each assignment adds a new property.

- Each refi strengthens your cash flow.

- Each sale restores your entitlement for the next

buy.

This is how service members retire with both pensions and portfolios.

Golden Nugget Tips

- **Always buy with an exit strategy.** Rent ratios and local demand matter more than curb appeal.

- **Use a spreadsheet, not emotion.** Run the numbers: cash flow, taxes, maintenance, and vacancy.

- **Don't overleverage.** A strong portfolio is one you can hold through rate swings and market dips.

- **Think like an investor, not a homeowner.** Comfort matters less than cash flow once you PCS.

The PCS investor isn't chasing houses; they're building assets that pay them back for years. Each set of orders becomes another opportunity, another stream of income, another piece of the financial puzzle. But even with all this opportunity, many service members still get trapped not by the system, but by misinformation.

Let's break that cycle.

Chapter 9

Avoiding the Traps

For every service member who used the VA loan to build wealth, there are ten who didn't, not because they couldn't, but because they were told the wrong information.

Sometimes it came from a lender who didn't specialize in VA loans. Sometimes it came from a well-meaning friend or relative. And sometimes, it came from within our own fear of getting it wrong.

But here's the truth: Most of the financial pain veterans experience in real estate doesn't come from bad markets. It comes from bad information.

Trap #1: "You can only use your VA loan once."
This one has cost service members millions in missed opportunities. The VA loan is *reusable*. Once your previous VA-financed property is sold or the loan paid off, your entitlement is restored, meaning you can buy again, and again, and again.

Even better? You can hold **multiple VA loans at the** same time if you have enough remaining entitlement. It's not about how many times you use it; it's about how smartly you use it.

Trap #2: "You have to be active duty to qualify."

Wrong. The VA loan benefit extends to:

- Active-duty service members
- Veterans
- National Guard and Reserve members (with qualifying service)
- Certain surviving spouses

In other words, your eligibility doesn't disappear when you hang up the uniform. It just shifts from active duty entitlement to veteran entitlement, and that distinction can last a lifetime.

Trap #3: "The VA loan is harder to get approved for."

Actually, it's often easier. VA loans are government-backed, meaning the lender has less risk, not more.

That allows for:

- No down payment
- More flexible credit standards

- No PMI (Private Mortgage Insurance)

When a lender says, "VA loans are too complicated," what they're really saying is, *they're not confident in doing them.* Find lenders who know the process cold. People who do VA loans every day, not just occasionally. Because the right lender isn't just processing your paperwork; they're protecting your entitlement.

Trap #4: "You can't buy an investment property."

Technically, the VA loan is for primary residences. But that doesn't mean it can't become part of your investment plan.

Here's how the smart ones play it:

- Buy as your residence first.
- Live there for at least a year (meeting VA occupancy requirements).
- PCS or move, then rent it out.

That's perfectly legal, and it's how thousands of service members quietly build rental portfolios over their careers. The trap isn't the rule; it's the misunderstanding of it.

Trap #5: "You can't assume a VA loan unless you're a veteran."

Another myth that's kept sellers and buyers alike from realizing their full potential. In reality, any qualified buyer, veteran or not, can assume a VA loan. The difference lies in *how* the entitlement is handled.

- If a **veteran** assumes and substitutes entitlement, the seller's entitlement is restored.

- If a **non-veteran** assumes, the seller's entitlement stays tied to the loan until it's paid off or refinanced.

Either way, the seller wins because assumptions can unlock higher prices and faster sales, especially when rates are high.

Trap #6: "Refinancing resets your loan benefits."

Not true. A VA IRRRL (Interest Rate Reduction Refinance Loan) doesn't reset your benefits. It's a *continuation* of your original entitlement. You're simply modifying the terms of the loan, not starting from scratch. This is where misinformation often costs homeowners tens of thousands.

A single point drop in interest rate could save you hundreds per month, but if you think refinancing "uses up" your VA benefit, you'll miss that opportunity entirely.

Trap #7: "You'll lose money if you sell too soon."

This one has half-truth to it. Yes, selling too soon can eat into your profit because of closing costs, commissions, and limited appreciation. But when done strategically, such as when offering an assumable loan in a high-rate market, selling early can actually *increase* your return. The trick isn't how long you own the home; it's *how* you sell it.

Trap #8: "Buying is risky; renting is safer."

Let's be honest. Renting *feels* safer because it's simpler. No maintenance, no market worries, no long-term commitment. But here's the real risk: you're still paying a mortgage, just not yours.

Renting is guaranteed negative cash flow. You lose 100% of your payment every month with zero return. Meanwhile, your homeowner counterpart is gaining equity, tax benefits, and appreciation, often using the same BAH. The question isn't whether buying has risk. It's whether you're okay funding someone else's retirement plan.

The Bigger Problem: Fragmented Information

Even with all the resources out there, military families often get fragmented advice:

- The lender focuses on rates.

- The realtor focuses on the transaction.

- The VA focuses on eligibility.

No one connects the dots between finance, strategy, and wealth-building. That's where education comes in and why this book exists. Because when you understand how all the pieces fit together, the system stops working against you and starts working *for* you.

Golden Nugget Tips

- Don't take advice from someone who's never used the VA loan themselves.

- Check your Certificate of Eligibility (COE) before assuming anything about your limits.

- Always verify lender claims. Not all lenders are VA-approved, and not all approved lenders are experienced.

- Misinformation costs more than interest. It costs years of opportunity.

The difference between the frustrated veteran and the financially free one isn't income; it's information. The first listens to myths. The second learns the rules and plays to win. And to prove it, let's look at real people who did exactly that. Veterans who used the same benefits you have, but with the right knowledge, built equity, freedom, and legacy.

Chapter 10

Real Case Studies

Theory is one thing. But stories, real stories, are what make this real. Because sometimes you don't need another formula or breakdown. You just need to see what it looks like *when someone like you wins.*

So let's look at three service members who turned their benefits into leverage using the same VA loan you already have access to. Different ranks. Different paths. Same playbook.

Case Study 1: The Assumption Advantage – How a Low Rate Sold Above Market

Rank: Staff Sergeant (E-6)

Location: Oahu, Hawaii

When Staff Sergeant Daniels received PCS orders to the mainland, he faced a common challenge selling his home in a high-interest market. Most sellers panicked when rates spiked from 3% to over 6%. Buyers couldn't afford as much house, and listings sat for months. But SSG Daniels had something special: a VA loan at 2.75%.

Instead of viewing it as an obstacle, he and his agent marketed it as a selling feature. The headline on his listing? *"Assumable VA Loan – 2.75% Interest Rate."*

That single line changed everything. Buyers lined up, including non-veterans, because they understood the math. The assumable loan dropped their potential monthly payment by over $1,500 compared to current rates.

After three weeks, SSG Daniels received multiple offers and sold for $15,000 above asking price, not because of upgrades or staging, but because he was offering something buyers couldn't get anywhere else: *affordability*. That's what happens when you know your loan is part of your leverage.

Case Study 2: The PCS Investor. Turning BAH into Cash Flow

Rank: Chief Warrant Officer (CW2)

Location: Colorado Springs → Virginia Beach

When Warrant Officer Jenkins PCS'd from Colorado to Virginia, he debated selling his first home. Instead, he ran the numbers. His mortgage was $2,350/month.

Rent in the area averaged $2,800. After property management and reserves, he still cleared around $250/month in positive cash flow, all while his tenants were paying down his loan.

He bought another home at his new duty station using his remaining entitlement and BAH to cover the new mortgage. Five years later, both properties had appreciated. The first was now worth $120,000 more than he paid. Jenkins refinanced it into a conventional loan, restored his VA entitlement, and bought a third property using the VA loan again.

By his 13th year of service, he had:

- Three properties across two states.

- Over $350,000 in combined equity.

- A clear path to retire with passive income.

He didn't flip houses. He didn't become a landlord guru. He just used every PCS as a chance to build, not reset.

Case Study 3: The Dual Benefit Spouse Strategy and Shared Entitlement

Rank: Lieutenant + Veteran Spouse

Location: Jacksonville, Florida

This couple played the long game. When they married, both had VA eligibility. Instead of combining it, they decided to alternate usage. One spouse buys using their entitlement while the other keeps theirs untouched.

They bought their first home for $310,000 using the husband's entitlement, then PCS'd three years later. The home became a rental, earning $400/month in positive cash flow.

At the next duty station, they used the wife's entitlement to buy their second property. When they sold the first home years later, they restored the husband's benefit and purchased another.

By alternating entitlements, they stacked properties without ever hitting a cap or running out of eligibility. Together, they turned two sets of benefits into a mini real estate portfolio before either of them reached retirement.

What These Stories Prove

None of these service members started with large savings, real estate experience, or deep connections. They started with what you already have, the VA loan, and added knowledge. They didn't just use it once and move on. They learned to reuse, refinance, and re-strategize.

That's the real secret to wealth in the military. Not luck. Not timing. Not rank. *Strategy*.

Golden Nugget Tips from the Field

- **Market your rate, not your price.** A low interest rate is worth more than granite countertops.

- **Use your PCS as your portfolio play.** Every move is an opportunity to expand, not reset.

- **Married service members can double their leverage.** Alternate entitlements to stack properties.

- **Keep great records.** You'll need them to restore entitlement and refinance smoothly later.

- **Your benefit is reusable.** Once you sell or refinance, it's not gone; it's reset.

The VA loan isn't just a financing option; it's a blueprint for mobility-based wealth.

Every PCS, every promotion, and every change of station can become another strategic move on your financial map.

And now that you've seen what's possible, let's break it down into pure action.

Chapter 11

Golden Nuggets: VA Loan Power Moves

By now, you've seen how powerful the VA loan really is, not just as a homeownership benefit, but as a *financial weapon*. This chapter is your **field guide,** the quick-access playbook you can come back to again and again. These are your **power moves,** the "Did you know?" strategies that separate the buyers who just use their benefit from those who *build with it*.

Golden Nugget #1: You Can Have More Than One VA Loan

You don't have to sell your first VA-financed home to use your benefit again. If you have remaining entitlement and qualify with your debt-to-income ratio, you can hold multiple VA loans at once, even across different states.

Pro move: Use this to build a portfolio one PCS at a time.

Golden Nugget #2: Your VA Loan Is Assumable, Even by Non-Veterans

Anyone can assume a VA loan (as long as they qualify with the lender). When rates rise, that assumption becomes gold: a low monthly payment that makes your property stand out. *Pro move:* Advertise your interest rate when selling. It's often worth more than a price drop.

Golden Nugget #3: Reuse It, Don't Lose It

Once your VA loan is paid off or the property is sold, your entitlement is restored, meaning you can use it again. It's not a one-time deal. It's lifetime leverage.

Pro move: File for entitlement restoration right after closing to keep your benefit ready for your next move.

Golden Nugget #4: The IRRRL Is Your Secret Weapon

The **Interest Rate Reduction Refinance Loan (IRRRL)** is the VA's easiest refinance option. No appraisal. No income check. Minimal paperwork. Use it to lock in a lower rate or stabilize your payment.

Pro move: When rates drop 0.75% or more, check your IRRRL options. The savings compound fast.

Golden Nugget #5: Split Your Entitlement Between

Spouses

If both you and your spouse are eligible, you can alternate whose entitlement you use. That lets you buy PCS, rent, and repeat without waiting for entitlement to restore.

Pro move: Create a two-person investment rhythm: one buys, one holds. Double your real estate reach.

Golden Nugget #6: You Can Rent Out Your Home After a PCS

The VA's occupancy rule only requires you to *intend* to live in the home for 12 months. After that, you can rent it out freely and keep the loan's favorable terms.

Pro move: Turn your previous home into a rental when you PCS. Let tenants pay your mortgage while you build equity.

Golden Nugget #7: No PMI, Ever

Private Mortgage Insurance (PMI) is what conventional buyers pay when they don't put 20% down. VA buyers? They skip it entirely, saving hundreds every month.

Pro move: Compare total payments, not just interest rates. The lack of PMI gives you more buying power.

Golden Nugget #8: You Can Refinance Non-VA Loans into a VA Loan

If you have a conventional or FHA loan, you can refinance it into a VA loan for better terms as long as you meet eligibility requirements.

Pro move: Use this to consolidate debt or drop PMI while securing the VA's lower rate structure.

Golden Nugget #9: Seller Credits Can Cover Closing Costs

VA buyers can negotiate **up to 4%** of the purchase price in seller credits covering closing costs, prepaid taxes, or even debt payoff.

Pro move: Use seller credits to buy down your rate or pay off high-interest loans before closing.

Golden Nugget #10: You Can Reclaim Entitlement After Divorce or Co-Ownership Sales

If your ex-spouse or co-owner refinances the home out of your VA loan, your entitlement can be restored.

You don't lose it forever; you just need to document the release.

Pro move: Always confirm your entitlement status after major life events.

Golden Nugget #11: Refinancing Doesn't Reset Your Entitlement

VA refinances like IRRRLs don't use new entitlement. They build on your existing one. That means you're still eligible for restoration later.

Pro move: Refinance with confidence. You're not using your benefit twice.

Golden Nugget #12: Property Type Matters, But Flexibility Exists

You can buy single-family homes, condos, duplexes, triplexes, or even fourplexes as long as you occupy one unit.

Pro move: Buy a fourplex, live in one unit, and rent out the rest. Let your tenants pay your mortgage.

Golden Nugget #13: The Funding Fee Isn't Forever

If you have a VA disability rating of 10% or higher, you're **exempt** from the funding fee, saving thousands at closing.

Pro move: File for your rating early if you're eligible. The savings add up over every transaction.

Golden Nugget #14: Equity = Freedom

Your mortgage payment builds equity. Refinancing

or selling smartly lets you **use that equity** to fund future purchases or investments.

Pro move: Use equity to buy assets, not toys. The right reinvestment compounds your wealth.

Golden Nugget #15: You Can Combine VA and Conventional Loans

In some cases, you can hold a VA loan and a conventional loan at the same time, which is useful when you're scaling across markets.

Pro move: Keep your VA loan for your lowest-rate property, and use conventional loans for expansion.

Golden Nugget #16: The VA Loan Isn't Charity It's a Reward

You earned it. It's not a handout; it's the result of service and sacrifice. When you use it strategically, you're honoring that effort by turning benefits into legacy.

Pro move: Treat your VA benefit like an asset, not a gift. Use it intentionally, not emotionally.

Golden Nugget #17: The VA Loan Can Build Generational Wealth

Every payment you make, every property you keep,

and every move you leverage builds something bigger than yourself: a future for your family.

Pro move: Name your properties. Literally. Make each one a milestone in your family's legacy journey.

The VA loan isn't about owning one home; it's about owning your future. It's not just for now; it's for *what's next.* And when you understand that you realize the goal isn't just to use your benefits wisely; it's to make them *last forever.*

Chapter 12

The Legacy Loop

There's a moment in every service member's life when the uniform comes off, and the question hits:

"What now?"

For years, the mission was clear: serve, lead, execute. But financial freedom is another kind of mission, one that doesn't end with your service. It continues if you choose to let it. And that's where the Legacy Loop begins.

The Loop of Service and Stewardship

The VA loan isn't a one-time benefit. It's a lifetime tool, a revolving door of opportunity you can open again and again. Every time you buy, sell, refinance, or assume, you're not just making a transaction; you're building *momentum*. It's the loop that starts with service and ends with stewardship. You served your country; now you can serve your family's future. When you use your benefits with intention, not impulse, you're transforming military service into *multi-genera-tional wealth.*

Your Wealth Is a Continuation of Duty

The discipline that made you effective in uniform structure, patience, and planning. Those same habits build wealth. The military trains us to prepare for contingencies, anticipate risks, and execute with precision. That mindset applies perfectly to financial freedom. You don't need to chase the next big thing. You just need to keep doing what you've always done: follow the mission, stay consistent, and adapt as conditions change. Each property, each move, each refinance are all part of your operational plan for prosperity.

From Ownership to Legacy

The goal isn't just to own homes; it's to own *outcomes.* Your VA loan can do more than house your family; it can house your legacy. Imagine your child using the rental income from your first home to pay for college. Or your grandkids learning about credit, equity, and discipline because they grew up watching you build something lasting.

That's legacy. Not wealth that fades, but wisdom that compounds. Because the real inheritance isn't the property. It's the pattern. It's the mindset of ownership, education, and stewardship that lives on long after you're gone.

The Freedom Dividend

Most people measure freedom by how much money they make. You'll measure it by how many choices you have. The VA loan gives you a foundation, but your actions give it direction. Whether you're 25 or 55, you can still turn that benefit into leverage.

Because freedom isn't built overnight. It's built every time you choose ownership over convenience, strategy over impulse, and purpose over panic. The sooner you start, the stronger your loop becomes.

Golden Nugget Mindset

- Service earned the benefit. Stewardship multiplies it.
- The uniform changes; the mission doesn't.
- Every home you buy should tell a story of progress.
- Teach your family what you learn. That's how legacy becomes culture.
- You didn't just earn a benefit. You earned a blueprint.

Your Final Mission

You've learned how to use your entitlement, assumptions, refinancing, and strategy to build wealth. Now it's about doing what every great leader does leaving the next generation better prepared than you were.

That's the Legacy Loop:

- You serve.
- You learn.
- You build.
- You teach.
- You pass it on.

And when that cycle repeats, when your kids see ownership as normal and wealth as responsibility, that's when your service truly pays off. Because the greatest rank you'll ever earn isn't in your military record. It's the one your family gives you when they look back and say, "They didn't just serve their country; they built our future."

Remember knowledge is leverage.
Need answers? Just Ask Antwaun.

Epilogue

Full Circle

If you made it this far, you're not just reading; you're *ready*. You've seen what's possible with the VA loan, and hopefully, you've realized this book was never about real estate alone. It's about perspective. It's about taking what you've earned, the benefit, the discipline, and the mindset and using it to build something permanent.

I didn't grow up knowing this stuff. Like many of you, I learned the hard way by missing opportunities I didn't even know existed. The goal of this book isn't just to teach you what I learned. It's to make sure you never have to say, *"If only I knew this sooner."*

The VA loan isn't a gift. It's a gear. one that keeps turning as long as you keep moving forward. Use it, refine it, share it. And when the next generation asks how you did it, tell them the truth: "I learned to make my benefits work for me, and now they'll work for you."

That's the real win when your service becomes a cy-cle of growth, and your financial freedom becomes your family's foundation.

- You've got the tools.
- You've got the strategy.
- Now go execute the mission.

About The Author

Antwaun Hill is a U.S. Army veteran and Hawaii-based real estate professional who's helped countless military families turn their benefits into wealth.

After serving 13 years in the Army and another decade as a Department of Defense contractor, he discovered a truth that changed his life: "Financial freedom isn't earned through rank; it's built through strategy."

Through his brand Ask Antwaun, he's become a leading voice in VA loan education, teaching service members how to leverage BAH, entitlement, and PCS cycles to build equity, ownership, and legacy.

His "BAH Means Buy A House" movement has inspired thousands to stop renting, start investing, and take control of their financial missions.

When he's not helping families navigate homeownership or writing his next guide, you'll find him mentoring fellow veterans, spending time with his family, and building his own legacy one property at a time.

Need real estate answers? Just Ask Antwaun.

 AskAntwaun@gmail.com

---

Ready to put your plan in motion? Scan below to set up your free strategy session with Antwaun Hill.

Other books in this series

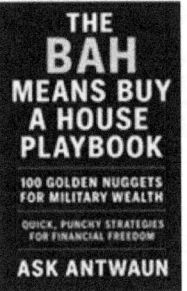